I0459173

KINSMAN AVENUE PUBLISHING, INC.
www.kinsmanquarterly.org

Registered with the U.S. Library of Congress
Library of Congress Control Number: *pending*

Printed in the United States of America

The Sin of Being Okay
Author: Dawn Leas

Cover Design: Summer Greigh
Author photo: Nathan Summerlin

THE
SIN
OF BEING
OKAY

DAWN LEAS

*For my grandmothers, mothers, aunts, sisters,
and cousins, by blood and chosen. May you know your
strength. And when you don't, may you be surrounded by
those who do.*

Table of Contents

...

I woke up at 3 a.m. thinking I was somewhere else

The air hasn't taken the turn
toward fall quite yet.

I want to be a tree blowing in wind.
I want to be the last leaf to fall, bright orange.

No. I want to be crimson.

Dreams are moving
against the jet stream.

A white-grey sky
carries hidden stories.

Maybe if I had a daughter,
I would know the secrets of this land.

Mom of grown sons,
I frequently stand on the sidelines.

How often can a heart skip
a beat and still go on?

Sometimes, I can hear the ocean
in the mountain wind.

Maybe the air has turned.
Maybe I can no longer feel variations.

Remember Etch-a-Sketches?
A quick shake would erase a life.

I miss cardboard playhouses,
Zoom and *Electric Company* –

my mom's fried chicken,
the greasy paper bags she used to bread it.

I can see the leaves are dimming
before their turn.

The water tower is dismantled.
I pray the church steeple doesn't topple.

This is how it ends

Unseasonable warmth.
Rain. No snow.
Fog. Hiss of tires
on wet pavement.
Wispy wind.

Dunkin Donuts
at the top of Moosic Street.
Fake stone facade.
Dim parking lot.
Blast of artificial light inside.
Imitation flavor shots.

Two cups in center
of brown Formica table.
Lids off to release the heat.
Steam shows off
stunning acrobatic display.

Evaporates.

A Positive Test

You knew the night you said yes. That night with no lights,
a cardboard nightstand with delicate pink flowers. Twin bed.
Second-floor apartment with bay window. A fire escape outside
the kitchen. You tried to leave the year before. Two months
of away-ness. Crying. The getting back together. Plans
for after graduation. You were a dreamer, a rule follower.
A reader of stories with happy endings. But, that night you
cooked dinner. That night, he helped wash dishes. That night
you undressed. (Look at you, playing adult.) And after, you
dressed again. After, you held hands while driving to meet
friends. After, your legs touched, your fingers curled
around his during the movie. Outside, you were a rainbow.
Inside, an electrical storm. You knew. Deep-down tiredness
during film criticism class. Waves of nausea while pouring milk
over Cheerios. Unmarried. Rule breaker. Playing house turned
real bills. Studying after bath time. Baby in infant seat
next to classroom desk. Laundry and dinner dishes. Argument
ending in *fuck you* (said to you, not by you, at least that first
time). But, you would show everyone you weren't a failure.
Not a statistic. You would build a happy life. Baby One. Baby
Two. A Family. You would be the good wife. Until you weren't.

The House on Frink Street

Decades-old Lincoln Logs smell
like wood right off the saw,
the new after heartbreak,
the before long silences.

A reminder of all those times
of trying to build a perfect home.
Failing one log after another. I used
to sit on the floor for hours, weeks

with my sons crouched in Fisher
Price pajamas covered in trains.
One's red curls, always akimbo,
back lit by winter sun. The other's

a white-blond mess of matchsticks.
They parked cars outside our play
home while the chinking I mixed
crumbled. Wood on wood. Friction

wore me down to a nub. I chanted
(to myself, others). *Wife. Mother.*
Beyond that, *who was I?* The air
smelled of melancholy the color

of Wegmans' apple juice. Not even
the red Crayola sippy cups breathed
light into the room. The tussle of boys
over a remote, explosion noises

as they kick and toss logs, beginning chords
of *Thomas the Tank Engine* kept me
from demolishing the house on Frink Street.

How to survive as a houseplant if you live with a beginner

Stretch daily until you touch
the ceiling. Befriend neighbors
with fast-growing vines. Spend
afternoons on wide sills
flirting with the sun. Invite first
blasts of heat to kiss your leaves.
Be patient, but ask for water
before you need it. Change. Welcome
the breath of the beginner tending
you. Listen. Keep her secrets.
Cultivate dreams of a successful
green thumb. One she didn't inherit.
Hold her fears. Change again.
Be slow to outgrow your home.

The Sin of Being Okay
A cadralor

1.
You drew triangles, circles,
squiggly lines in margins above
math problems with purple pen,
under reading notes. Teachers
expected answers you couldn't
find outside the windows past
the flat playground, horse farms
and cow pastures, just
the tip of your imagination.

2.
He dreams in tie-dye
each bright yellow flowing
into pink, green, blue, orange.
He sees *dream you* before *real you*
teased hair, Rugby shirt
three sizes too big. *Real you*
rarely smiles, worry lines
setting into forehead. But his voice
reaches you, unfolds your mouth.

3.
How you describe the color of water –
blueberry, shallow as
your grandmother's eyes, violet
like your cousin's middle name,
blue as a marble skittering
across terrazzo in mid-summer sun.
Muted trumpet in a city club.
Your favorite pair of Levi's decades old.
A lover's voice saying, *I'm sorry*.

4.
Define sinoky –
Sin of being okay.
Collage of photos with faded edges.
Lying naked in the woods.
Late-spring snow.

Gold star for breaking the rules.
Crying during sex.
A dream that can be let go.
A period with hot flashes.
Underwater sounds of an abandoned ocean.

5.
From an early age
you learned to be small
could fit in a Jack-in-the-Box
at the slightest raised voice,
even brief eye contact, embarrassing
hair out of place. Each person
cranked – one click, two clicks, three.
The tighter the turn, the tinier
you became until the pop splintered your life.

Groceries for One

I'm wandering the aisles of Wegmans
on autopilot with an army
of after-work shoppers –

one cart has a quart of milk,
a bag of lettuce and two apples.
A woman in a suit has a basket
brimming with Amy's Kitchen.

I grab a family-sized tub
of spring mix, a gallon of Lactaid.
two boxes of yogurt popsicles,
and four boxes of quinoa pasta.

The cost is high.

When the boys were little,
we shopped on Thursdays –
a big outing to town for us.
They strained against seat
belts as I pushed them
in a cart masquerading as a car.

I just wanted them safe.

We fought over junk food.
I gave in to Matchbox cars

yet always worried about the cost of things.

Now, I'm waiting for one son
to return from the Wisconsin woods
where the ticks are infected with Lyme.
I'm praying the other one back
from the center of a black hole.

I'm imagining what it would be like to live alone.

I half-listen to music on the drive
home, lug groceries
and my work bag
into the house, throw mail

on kitchen table. Sinking
into the sofa I watch
House Hunters International,
eat chips with sour cream for dinner.

Gone

You pour coffee into Dr. Who mug,
add just enough milk, one level
teaspoon of sugar. Stir and stir
until last granules dissolve. Stand
back. Wait for the heat to do its work,
spark a chemical reaction,
warm cold porcelain. Sigh
as Tardis fades in increments –
ghost shadow to no trace.

You can relate.

An hour after he leaves for work,
the Tardis is back.
A small puddle stains
bottom of mug.

Tangible signs everything
that leaves eventually returns.

But does he notice you fading
week by month by year
like coffee steam billowing
in a breeze
the kitchen window let in
until his good wife is gone... gone... gone?

Meteor Shower

Tempel-Tuttle takes her time orbiting the sun.
Slow, but fierce. Leaves her signature
and when Earth crosses her path –
       an orchestrated show of light.

Just before dawn,
you lie on the concrete sidewalk
five hours behind the East Coast
a symphony of birds
singing the morning awake.

You snap pictures of Jupiter, Venus and Mars,
the distance between immeasurable with just the eye.

Then Leonid's radiant falls through the constellation Leo
and the shower changes everything.

I ask when you'll be home.
You answer, *right quick.*

Just after midnight,
I lie down on a cold driveway
dead leaves scratching its surface.
Above me, pines and red oaks tip-toe
their way to the northern sky.

My Scorpio lives by the moon.
       Has a hard time forgetting.
Your Aries lives close to the edge of Mars.
We will forgive each other for this every day.

The comet lumbers along.
The meteor shower comforts.
Mother Earth spins.

Right quick takes on new meaning
in space. Thirty-three years to orbit
just once? We are experts at waiting.

Good Girls

learn the difference
between second
and third bases
from older girls
while listening
to *Tapestry*
in the back bedroom
of a drafty duplex,
parents' hushed talk
floating up through
the floor vents.

Good girls write
Mrs. Houdak
with fancy curlicues
in the back
of their Mead binders,
marry first loves.

Good girls don't play
Spin the Bottle,
hearts racing
in the back
of a coat closet,
don't even think
about strip poker.

Good girls don't do
7 a.m. walks of shame,
or hang on front porches
with frat boys
drinking and smoking,
but go to Confession
on Saturday afternoons,
receive Communion
on the tongue
not in palm of hand.

Good girls sew
Power Ranger
Halloween costumes,
bake from scratch,
chaperone first-grade
field trips
to the Baltimore Aquarium.

Good girls don't accelerate
through yellow lights,
don't allow pre-teen sons
to grow hair past shoulders
or listen to Metallica.

Good girls don't long
for afternoons alone,
apartments in the city,
dream jobs on the West Coast,
endless dancing at concerts,
the smell of men
who are not their husbands.

Naming Nail Polish

Friends dreamed of decorating classrooms,
marathon study sessions in a law library,
being sleep deprived on clinical rotations
so they could catch babies, set bones.

They imagined heading upstate
to learn how to caramelize and slice,
turn food into art, own a Michelin
3-star restaurant. Working their way
from teller to branch manager.

Practicing perms and hair dye
to *Beauty School Drop-Out*.
Hopping a bus and not going home
until armed with a bevy of Tonys.
I dreamed of learning the ways
of New Orleans, raising children
on beignets and bayous. Hitching
a trailer to a red F-150. Boots and Levi's.
Heading south on I-35 out of Denton.
Weekends of barrel racing. I still dream

of a windowless office in a building made
of glass and steel. Research in my job title.
A lab table of my very own. Black Sharpie
and clipboard. Daily palettes of the rainbow.

Glittery. Glossy. Moody matte.
Marshmallow.
Milky Way.
Meandering Heart.

I'm not Dawn Colangelo anymore

Inside Northeast Title & Tag,
we stand shoulder to shoulder.
The line holds us up.

Clip-art flyers taped to fake wood paneling.
Plastic chairs in a compact space,
people hoping for smooth transactions.
From overhead speaker
comes NPR poetry -

lines from "Patty's Charcoal Drive-In"
mingle with your words
telling me to sign my name
one last time.

The strip-mall sun blinds us.
We walk shoulder to shoulder.
Our cars, parallel lines.

You won't look at me.
I unhinge.

Earlier that week, I visited
our house, packed more boxes.
Your to-do list on the fridge
includes *forgive Dawn Colangelo.*

When our marriage was young,
I signed a receipt
Dawn Colangelo. You looked
over my shoulder and said
that isn't your name anymore.

Now, here you are changing me back.

Outside Northeast Title & Tag,
there's something about the stale summer wind –
how it gathers mini-twisters of dust,
how it lifts what others left behind
            making empty bags and used cups dance together
that gives me back my voice to spin and spit –
look at me, look at me.

Jersey Girl

Spring trying to rise from the horizon. Porta-Potty lines 50
deep. My cousins and I jump up and down to stay warm, watch
runners in shorts and tank tops do warm-ups sprints. We inch
closer to the front of the line, take turns holding water bottles,
share hand sanitizer. My cousin takes a group selfie to share.
I aim toward the sky wearing a shawl of grey. We find our back-
of-the-pack corral. Shuffle, walk, slow jog until our feet land on
rubber mat. Chip activated. We pace slow as a honey those first
few miles. Listen to conversations compete all around us.
A beef recall. Someone's mom and *E.coli*. Where to eat after
half marathon. I catch snippets, will my brain to hold on for a
poem later, but lose them somewhere around mile six. We walk
water stations. I eat watermelon-flavored energy beans. I watch
mile markers 7, 8, 9... I slow down to stretch, tell them to go
ahead. Their bobbing heads, green tech shirts disappear.

Waves race to the shore,
white-capped and ready to rest
Springsteen sings me home.

Birthday Eve

The night before your 27th birthday,
there's no covert wrapping frenzy
in a walk-in closet.
No checking off party-planning tasks,
or last-minute runs to the store.

Like when you were on the edge
of three declaring you wanted a red party.
Plates and napkins; pizza and Kool-Aid.
A Winnie-the-Pooh pirate cake.
The must-wear-red-to-attend invite.

All these years
between your tow-head turning
ash blond. Your voice dropping
deep as a well.

This year, there will be no cake,
no quick trip to New York. You on the other
side of the continent now. At least there is only
land, lake, and mountains that divide us

unlike those dark years – blankets
of silence, heavy as wet snow.

Those phone calls from a stranger.
An R.A. just doing his job for free board
announcing you were somewhere
I couldn't reach.

Your turn toward light.

And then when my own storm
lifts me into a tornado, your voice
pulling me back to ground.

I'm tired of telling the story...

the one that ends happily
for just one of us. What
can I ask of you other than
to be the opposite of me?

In this world of do-the-right-thing,
and always-follow-the-rules,
I'm too tired to do anything,
but break the vows
we said before we could read.
Not that you ever loved reading.
Especially poetry. We tried

for years too many to count
until I shed *wife,*
and you shrugged off *husband.*

No, let's be honest, I stripped
you of that mourning –
leaving us to squirm
when someone asked *what happened?*

When we start the dance of Paris,
the city we never visited together,
we each wonder why we gave
so many decades to fighting
about the details of our fairy tale
that didn't end happily ever after
but in courthouse news.

There was no public wake,
but I light a candle for you
every night to erase the words
I don't like and you don't know.

After I Leave My Husband

Rain for three years now.
This week, downpours
drum on an anniversary of ending.

It's hard not to sink in the muck.
Trees, bushes and grass
verdant and alive as can be.
He and I, dead three years now.
The sky shifts from woolen comfort to charcoal concern.

When I'm making lunch,
when I'm alone,
I listen to "Grey Street" on repeat,
remember the DMB concerts I heard it live
thinking *this is me.*

The grey reaches my grown son in the city.
I sit in the mountains
listening to his heavy words mix
with angry cars, angrier people
as he walks from midtown to the Village,
wanders Bushwick.

I remember navigating the Delaware
Water Gap as my teenage son
asks the question I've been waiting
for his whole life.
When I say yes, he's quiet before

　　　　it's hard to wrap my head
around the thought that my existence
changed the course of two lives.

I hold the wheel tight.
Look at him, back to the road.

I always wanted to be a mom.

I take a curve too quickly
as he looks out over the river.

A tornado touches down in my heart.

Trio

1. Construction/Deconstruction

We worked well together. He could eye a straight line with
laser-level precision and do mental math quicker than a blink.
I kept tidy piles, always stacked things symmetrically. I read
directions, followed them, mostly. We thought we were building
a fortress, one that would house us well into retirement.

One morning, to our surprise, we woke to find out we had read
the wrong plans. We hadn't built a fortress, but a wall. Between
us. One that was too high to climb, too large to break down, too
strong to break through. We worked well together.

....

2. Naming the Hurricane

Mid-life crisis
　　　　selfish
Peri-menopause
　　　　space
Childhood trauma
　　　　separation
Un-mended heart
　　　　single-mindedness
Broken vow
　　　　self-centered
Ennui
　　　　so you
Brain tumor, thyroid dysfunction, vitamin D deficiency –
　　　　science fails at explanation.
The first lightning strike is leaving,
and the wind whips up a funnel
　　　　of *it's you, not me*.

But wait until the sky torrents water
to name it

　　　　walking away.

....

3. Never did I…
> want to become a statistic,
> believe I would love living alone,
> imagine sitting across a conference table,
>> a lawyer between us,
> think I would break us apart like a wishbone.

In hindsight...
> the odds were against us,
> I was made for living alone,
> there had always been something between us,
> brittle eventually breaks.

If I told the end of our story in haiku, would you forgive me for everything?

When winter arrived, I was
just grateful you socked away
peanut butter. It

was enough to get
us through nothingness. Its shelf
life outlived us. When

I walked out the red
door, I didn't know how much
I would miss bleeding.

I've gotten far from
our real story – now you
hold me at arm's length.

I feel that in my
stomach, by the way. I want
to live on the edge

of evergreens. Cold front range.
No human sounds for weeks.
Not really. I'm not

a woman of the
forest. More salt air, water.
I want the rough bay.

Pirouetting white
caps I bobbed above, below,
the weight of guilt like

a baby on my hip.

Delta

I am a mosaic of Emerald Isle,
Italian leather and gypsy song.

I am swirls of magic,
stories my grandmother told in Slovak,
a language she lived in,
but never taught us.

I am salt. I am water.
Flowing blue to green,
dancing calm to chaos in a white foam dress.

I did not root in mountain mud
like an evergreen, but in sandy soil,
like a pitch pine or orchid
moving with fire and breeze
in the barrens of New Jersey.

I am the woman
stepping off the known trail
into the dunes, a mirage maze.

I am a delta,
where the Mississippi kisses the Gulf,
a slow approach to open water.

I am the horizon,
the intersection of water and sky.

How to come alive after a divorce
after Ada Limon

It's not bird song declaring we've made it to another day,
          last icicle dripping away,
          long-forgotten sun
          appearing earlier and staying later

or my twin counting down to early retirement,
          first run on the levee after a snowy
          winter, or children playing
          outside between school and dinner.

It's wild wind crying through years
          for a season lost before laughing
          with the arrival of a new one,
          wrapping itself in my hair

as rain drops, slowly at first, like a toddler's
          tentative first steps before bursting
          into a frenzied dance, its clean
          scent full of maybes and memories

of my grandparents' back yard on First Avenue
          dewy grass and damp dirt a makeshift
          court, a rim nailed high on a tree trunk
          the ball swishing through metal net.

Fusion

1.
Breathing in that thin air,
you rode a banana-seated bike
to the movies. Your mom sent
water bottles to quench altitude sickness.

I practiced y'all with a northern accent
over and over,
learned how not to drown
below sea level.

2.
The Carolina humidity hugged you,
almost to the point of suffocation.
Drought-cracked Texas
swallowed my voice.
The heat wave nearly boiled our goldfish.

3.
You were experimenting
with pony-tailed hair
and lyrics,
mind-altering substances.

I was experimenting
with being afraid of everything

but, I wanted to make rain purple
while my friends drank Rum and Coke,
set free the mystery rising from my toes,
licking my ribs, prickling my heart.

4.
It would take decades for us
to collide – a bundle of kinetic energy,
gravitational pull
toward the molecular cloud,
fusion a secret language
only our bodies could translate
into a luminous, new star all our own.

Monopoly

He walks into my life after I already used
my share of get-out-of-jail-free cards.
No wiggle room left for breaking rules,
time for good behavior taken off the table.

I step off the boardwalk. He follows.
We build a beach camp.
Draw up plans for a home on Park Place.
We tell childhood stories as the fire dwindles
make coffee to carry the conversation
until two a.m. I crochet a collection of scarlet
letters, tattoo one on the nape of my neck.
He traces it first with his fingers then lips.

The want drives me deep into the ocean
where I build an underwater monopoly.
Work is busy, but I keep an eye
on life on land. Scenes of him –
blueprints spread on sand, overseeing
construction on Park Place, showing
the old New York Avenue house
to a couple from Tennessee –
ripple with each wave turning over.

I send weightless words to the surface
riding the backs of air bubbles.
They pop before he reads them.
My hair turns to seaweed.
I grow a single fin, but no gills.
He swims at sunset.
Sits in the surf searching the horizon.
I don't ride a wave to land,
but swim toward the sun.
Only I can save myself from drowning.

Trowel, Screen, Camera

I never wanted to be an archeologist. Until I met you. Wide-brim
hat and hiking boots. Reach of the mid-summer sun long
over the Rockies. Dust of dry season and sweat staining back
of a linen shirt. Sleeves rolled up to my elbows. I crisscross
time zones searching your history. Traipsing across topographies,
I trowel Colorado sandstone. Sift soil through screens. I hike
the mountains of North Carolina with a backpack full of supplies.
Toggled metal bottle bounces off my hip with each step.
Listening to "Rhymes and Reasons" on repeat, I collect artifacts.
Your elementary school pictures. Home-movie footage of you
learning to skip. The last page of a high-school essay about Bowie.
Newspaper feature on your college band. A photo of you
with long-hair, lips just a millimeter from mic. First page of your
first screenplay. I dig and dig to learn who you are. Yes, I am
writing another poem to teach you who I am.

Living alone post-divorce during allergy season

After years of stale air – slow suffocation
between biting words and silence –

I want open windows always. A breeze for feathers
to ride. Rain-soaked grass. Neighborhood dogs.
Midnight argument outside Turkey Hill.

Distracted by pollen on every flat
surface, too stubborn to close windows,
I stockpile tissues to combat the green haze.

This suffering is better than central air,
so much better than keeping quiet.

The key to healing doesn't need
to be metal. It can be bamboo. A fan cooling
hot flashes. A salt lamp switched off each evening.

I know what's inside, what it takes to make it,
where to catch the updraft. That's enough for now.

Last Leaf in Fall

I remember –
         cobalt sky,
         curvaceous clouds,
         canopy of shade.

Not cling of humidity.
Not growl of traffic.
Not scratch of grass on back of legs.

I remember –
         your arugula and chickpeas,
         my romaine with sweet balsamic
                 zing of pepper,
         long draws of water.

I remember –
         talking but not the details,
         the timbre of your voice,
                 how you spoke with me,
                         not around, above, or through.

I remember –
         you clearing your throat before...
                 tell me something about Dawn.
         the pause...
                 a whoosh of air, seconds of silence,
         swirl of thoughts landing on *I don't know who I am.*

Not what I said. Not *I am a mom.* Not *I am a wife.*

                 I swayed
                 like the last leaf in fall
                 not wanting to let go.

I remember –
         tilt of a world now off kilter.

Spirit Animals

You dream a brass camel
into the palm of your hand.

I fly fourteen hours to ride one
in the Arabian desert.

He heaves and rocks to standing,
takes me deeper into the dunes,
the camp disappearing
into a sepia-toned mirage.

I beg the handler for more minutes,
the camel's height and sway
soothing.

I see answers in the orange sunset,
the cinnamon-colored haze,
feel them rise in the rhythm
of long, lean legs,
in the humps that carry enough water
for the entire dry season.

This desert wants me.
I may be falling in love.

Long before we met,
you dove deep into the Pacific
just off the coast of paradise,
an owl perched on a high cliff.

She flew across a continent
of years to deliver me to the desert.

Our spirit animals come from different lands,
but learn to work in tandem,
invent a new language

to guide us to evergreen trails,
desert dunes, a tropical rain forest.
Always back to salt water.
Places they know will save us.

We are traveling separately,
but in the same direction.

First Meeting

You, pony-tailed and tall.

Me, pixie-cut, a mouth
full of braces.

You reached
               across a library table.
I reached back, no eye contact.

You turned to talk
to another poet.

Me, a jumble of jitters
right before a public reading
turned to find a familiar face.

Later, you would say *aloof*
then smile.

Later, I would say *distant*
then shrug, *as if you didn't like me*.

It would take years
for a conversation
to glow hot,
spark the bonfire
that started our story.

we begin with pepper

In a packed booth,
my shoulder rests
against your arm.

You blanket your omelet
with coarse pepper.
I shower my salad with it.

I want some heat
on my tongue,
the spice of your lips
on my neck.

First familiar chords
blast from jukebox.

We get lost
between verse
and refrain

as our server trades
tray for mic,
jumps onto a half wall
to sing for tips.

Surrounded by music,
laughter, scrape of forks
on plates, I press
my thigh against yours.

We are the mouth
of a newborn fire.

Hiking

after Antonio Porta

Behind the words, can you hear my heart?
A low thrum of tension.

Tug of tears.
Years of pretending.

Your touch breaks
this chandelier of ache.

You sing my name
night after night.

When the singing doesn't work,
we go to the woods.

A new salve for me.
We take turns leading.

Is there a trail blaze to follow?
Is this rhododendron or mountain laurel?

I need to study plant life.
I need to learn how to not pretend.

After an hour of eyes down on mud, rock, grass,
I open my arms to the wind.

May Day

Three years divorced.
I'm not sure the ink has dried,

but I can breathe again.

I don't listen to jazz anymore
but crave
a whispering late into the night.

More prayer or meditation
than lament.

I dance at midnight
with a man
who welcomes my crying
over unseen galaxies.

We get lost driving through World's End,
a dirt road lined with trees
but aren't worried
about finding our way back.

He searches for landmarks.
I keep my eyes on the cresting hill.

Heartbreak

I'll tattoo the sky
with the heartbreak of a yes.
Declare it in the middle
of a packed stadium
bass reverberating
so you can't say it back.

It's no longer an option
to not talk my way
out of a hard corner.

That summer on the Cape.
In the bay.
Wind. Waves. Water.
I wanted to float out and out and away.
Almost did.
Just to feel jellyfish sting
of being found out.

What's the harm in going under water
to sing where no one can hear
the truth in my voice?

Tie me to you with seaweed.
I promise not to let go.

No wait. It was that song. The one
that tied our hearts together.

No wait. Tell your side
of the story. I like it better.

Let's take the bus.
Just you and me out West.

Salt flats.
Desert Arches.
Redwoods.

All the way to the ocean you like best.

Intersection

Remember how I wanted
into your world
so completely,
I hurricaned my life –
safe from any beast
other than myself.

The first act was a puzzle
riddled dialogue,
set changes tripping
over one another.

But, oh, that second act.

I found my way to the eye,
sent starlings out
to gather you.

It didn't surprise me
you rode in on lightning,
tumbled through turbulence.
It was quiet here.

You liked quiet.

The storm played
out in punctuated
strobes of light.

No one ever thought
to look for us here,
so we lived out life
under dark skies
called our shooting-star
offspring names
forgotten by sunrise.

Swimming at Little Beach

After parking in a crowded lot, trekking down a path
under an umbrella of trees, kicking off flip-flops to feel sand
on feet, looking at the horizon just past indigo waters
and seeing possibility, climbing a narrow path of rust-colored
rocks – using our hands – standing at the top breathless
over the view, navigating the hill down to more sand, I peel
off a t-shirt of shame, shorts of guilt, a bathing suit
of self-loathing and dive into that salty, salty water. It begins
to rain – the water almost clear, the air – a hint of tropical winter.
We swim separately before together. Bob with gentle waves,
duck under larger ones. You say something that makes me
smile. I float as the rain ends, my ears just under the surface
muffle your voice. I feel free. I am free.

Just Before Your Hair Caught Fire

A dirty horizon
not ready for April's
Pink Moon.

Queen of adaptation,
you'll make more with less.
Expectation a bridge
with so many locks
missing a key.

Don't jump in that river
murky with the sludge
of your heart.

Drowning is quicker
than finishing the story.

You never liked rivers.
Or the lakes
of your mountain home –
a size or blossom too big,
not soon enough for you.

Freedom always rides
the surge of snow melt,
but you were too afraid
to wade out, fight
the debris from upriver.

You colored between the lines
until you learned
your heart was made of glass.

First crack so tiny,
you didn't feel its spidering.
Didn't know
you could find a fix
until it webbed
beyond shadows
beyond the line
you thought you'd never cross
beyond words
and just before your hair caught fire.

Garden State Parkway

A Friday road race with limos and buses for a glimpse
of the full moon rising over black water. Early morning run past
Stone Pony in steady rain. Salt water and sand. Layers
of clouds like folds of a down comforter. Asbury Park memories
of grandparents, carousel rides, and twins in matching bucket
hats and blue Keds. Writing in a parlor with an ocean view.
Red sea glass. People watching on the boardwalk. Running
through Bradley Beach. Running through Avon-by-the-Sea.
Running. More waves. Words. Words. Words. Thank you. Fall.
A different life. Impatiens droop over sides of terra cotta pots.
They know it's time to go.

Elsewhere is where I want to be

Take one guilt off after the other,
a striptease of regret.

Let me start again.

Let me not pause
at the crossroads
of married and unmarried.

I want to buy a Beetle convertible,
put a real red daisy on the dash and go
to where the pain doesn't hum
all the damn time
just beneath the voice
that keeps saying *I'm ok*

until I'm choking on goodbyes
too many to list here.

My sons, when you look back
to those early summer calls –
me in my station wagon, mini-mart parking lot,
you both somewhere in the city –
I hope you hear what's underneath *I'm sorry.*

Then, hold on to my apron,
the one I never wore in your childhood,
maybe I can cook us up a fresh pot of life.

Haleakala

I like ocean views
and my air thin.
I wear clouds

as necklaces,
generate my own heat.
It's best you learn

my hazard zones. Stand
barefoot in my crater.
This is how

I'll teach you to never turn
your back. Don't mistake
silence for giving up.

There's a difference
between dormant
and extinct. Anger

no longer rises
in my throat, but still beats
steady at my core. I cheat

on the sun with the moon.
I cheat on the moon
with the sun. They pretend

not to know. I am a woman
who wants. Nothing
wrong with that.

Shopping at Giant

A June Sunday. Grocery day. Instead of Price Chopper west
of the Susquehanna, you're in the Green Ridge Giant just blocks
from your college apartment where you and your husband
conceived your first son. Your friend and you each take a cart.
Yours has a wobbly wheel, its vibration against tile rises
into the handle. Into your sweaty palms. You feel the frenetic
beat of your ears.

You meander produce. Try to remember what it's like to be
hungry. You want to fill a cart with comfort to batch-make
your mother's chicken soup, meatloaf with extra ketchup.
To fill a basement freezer with dated Glad containers to avoid
eating spoiled food. But on this day, you've properly spoiled your
marriage.

You can't remember your favorite foods. Ones you hate.
Can't remember a time of one rather than four or two. You palm
a beefsteak smooth as ice, lift it to your nose. Not quite as lush as
one plucked from Great-Grandma Szorocsin's garden,
but it'll do. Keep things simple. Leafy romaine. Chicken with
crisp, burnt skin. Green beans to bake drizzled with balsamic.
A cucumber to calm your stomach. Individual yogurts
for work lunches.

You twirl your rings as the registers beeps. Not quite single yet.
At least you can make your friend dinner. You can't imagine
when you'll be hungry again.

Ode to the first place I lived alone

You weren't dressed in shag carpeting
    or decorated in 70's harvest gold appliances.

You didn't smell of pot, weren't littered with drop cloths
    and paint cans, hammers, a table saw.

You weren't introduced to me by a woman in leopard-print
    sleep pants and black tank, a vape nestled in her cleavage.

You were airy as meringue. Plaster walls with new white paint
    and doors like a bodybuilder's neck. Windows with screens
    that let in the scent of fall rain.
    Your owner required three references and called each one.

You were built to survive. A flood that flowed
    through you uninvited, an angry fist in your wall,
    tenants who never appreciated your luxurious closets.

You smelled of just-installed carpeting, bathroom cleaner.
    Later, of pine or cucumber melon.
    Thieves or eucalyptus, sex and love.

You were quiet, still empty the first night we spent together.
    You and me, a backpack, garbage bag stuffed with clothes
    and towels. I slept on the bedroom floor
    with a comforter and pillow.

You never judged the boxes of books hauled up three flights
    to your built-ins, the fog I brought
    into your uncluttered space.

You believed in the fact that time didn't exist. That memory
    was bendable, that you could stitch my heart
    and de-clutter my mind. Soon I learned
    your strength. Soon you taught me how to survive.

Timed Door

Minneapolis Skyway

These twin cities don't look exactly the same.

Like you and your sister –
              her red hair to your brown.
She speaks with her right hand,
              you always go left.
Her scientific logic questions
              your emotional language.

She seeks wide fields –
              corn stalks swaying.
Her husband saves the hen house
from foxes roaming the night.

You want stacked, vertical living,
              one a.m. conversations
in a standing-room only bar.
              Sun rising over steel.

Stop there.

Choose your wings carefully
and tell her to do the same.
No need for separate exits –
you will fly together
to the Mississippi River of your childhood
              far south from here –
where you splashed each other,
ran away,
then toward one another
knowing your parallel paths will somehow cross on this skyway,
a labyrinth connecting the past to the present,
a sanctuary for you both.

You breathe in tandem like these cities
no matter how many miles are between you.
You know, she knows
where one ends and the other begins
even as the sky fills with snow.

Almost Spring

On the first day the corner cafe
props its front door with a chair,
you know you will survive.

With unzipped windows
and a pushed back sun roof,
you take the slow route between
Wilkes-Barre and Scranton.
A train whistles. Tires speak to pavement
pocked by leftover salt.

The radio pulls
you deeper
into the 80s
with "Rock with You,"
and "The River."

You pass Ghigarelli's Pizza
and remember the Old Forge
guys you've kissed –
one in the Chuck E. Cheese
parking lot in Dickson City,
the other in a crowded motel room
during senior week in Wildwood
both of you barely dressed,
bottles dangling from fingertips.

The last patches of snow hang
onto Montage Mountain
like acne on the face of a teenager.

You write at every red light,
pass the Taylor Walmart
where you shopped the morning
your water broke with your second son.

You see the house your friend
scraped and painted and decorated
to make just right until her husband left.
The new owners painted over her cherry
red front door with pea green.

This is the route you drove four times daily
when your boys were in elementary school –
fifteen miles of small towns stitched together
by bars, churches, strip malls, rows of houses
so close they feel each other breathe,
hear the secrets of their neighbors.

The recent past aches like a pulled muscle slow to heal,
a bruise that won't fade,
but this drive is untying the knots.

Crank the volume.
Take a long breath.
Pull to the side of the road
to begin the last line of this poem.
Gather your hair in a loose bun.
Continue to drive as slowly as speed limit will allow.

There's nothing heavier than a blank page

(maybe) waiting for a comet to drop
                        space dust.
                        You must be ready
                        with notebook open.

Not distracted by your love's tongue
tracing the ocean on your wrist.
                        You kiss with eyes open.
                        Toward the sky.
                        Waiting.

And when first sprinkles touch
                        your face,
                        blinking like fireflies,
                        you hold the notebook

above your head. An offering. The dust
forms letters, turns over into words.
                        It's your story,
                        but you don't know
                        the language.

Be completely honest here. You never
                        learned
                        to read. No
                        one ever knew.

Luckily, gusts of wind came
when it was your turn to read aloud.
                        Never mind.
                        You're a storyteller.
                        The moths say so.

Convince the cicadas doing everything
                              (except kissing)
                              with your eyes
                              closed always leads

to magic. The ants shake their heads
at the impracticality of this.

                              Their DNA rebels
                              against it.
                              There's too much

 to gather in this season. They keep
                              marching.
                              Save the creating
                              for first frost of fall.

A winter throwing ice.
The blank page is heavier
                              than anything else
                              in our known world.
                              Acceptance is critical.

Cicadas know this to be true
                              and settle
                              in for another
                              17-year night.

Ditto

Dare Paris to press her
simplicity into morning.

Chase away a cold snap
with a trip to Red Rock.

Teach me to pronounce
Hennepin, to follow the dust.

Fly to New Orleans or Dublin –
or where the rim of imagination meets your voice.

Tell me another fractured miracle,
one that's too little daring,
too much beautiful.

Independence

The rain comes every day for weeks. In giant bursts, droplets
breaking on tree branches. Often in drenching curtains the wind
blows west to east. The water pools muddied in the construction
site outside my office. I'm quickly giving up on summer.
You're saying you'll never let go. On the eve of the fourth
of July, it's dry. We drive over an hour to the middle
of nowhere for a softball game. There's a tractor parked outside
the Turbotville Great Valu and marked spots for buggies.
A young couple climbs into one. He's suspendered and bearded.
She's white-capped and long-dressed, unwrinkled. They look
full of hope. I think there's a poem here. I try to take pictures,
but my memory is full. You refrain from a lecture. My niece
throws strike after strike after strike in the bottom of the sixth.
The stands cheer. The next morning we wake to more rain.

Half Truths

It was the cusp of summer.
A loss lingering just around the bend.

Little did we know racing to navy water,
sand polka-dotted with cranberries
that the world was flat
and light arced. We breathed
in salty stories, hands and arms riding
the wind out windows.

The hill shook its towel, but sand
stood firm under deflated tires.

With no time to fasten seatbelts,
we somersaulted up and over
like a beach ball caught by a tailwind.

T.J. knew this was normal
his baritone stayed steady.
I questioned the history,
the dunes, my entire adult life
trying to stand on its head,
proving it right and me wrong.
Bea took copious notes. Her pencil worked
upside down, the umbrellas kept
her page from getting burned.

After three rotations,
the SUV landed upright on water.
The sand hung high in the sky.
A puzzle for us to sail to our mountain-locked home.

Next time, I'll wear fancier shoes,
pair them with straw hat.
T.J. will buy stock in hand sanitizer.
Bea will watch a keyboard write
her story – no effort needed.

Here's what I learned at the flat
edge of the world –
Always leave a lamp on,
a breadcrumb for friends
known to roll in after hours,
high on a wave of cool, white sand,
always cresting, always flowing,
occasionally ebbing

in all the wrong directions.

Let

your voice   out.

Off-key. Out of tune.
Doesn't matter.

Let it   out.

Until tears
seize your breath.

Until your screams
don't sound human.

Until your head hurts.

Because that's where
you'll know
you're a child

of salt water,
full moon

cloud-filled nights
in a Hungarian
town way out

in the country
where you've
never visited,
probably won't.

You are a city person.

Always want the choice
to keep a lamp
lit, run down
to a Bodega
for a pint of ice cream

to carry you
through the lonely hours,
the ones you prayed
into your life
because you just couldn't face

a decade more of idle chatter
half-hearted words,
silent road trips
when you counted
mile markers
you already knew from memory.

A route memorized
at a young age, one
you never thought
would lead
into this life set
on repeat

until you stopped the skip
of scratched records
you carried from state to state

until you said
nothing was a hell
of a lot better than empty

and you walked out
knowing you didn't know
which route to take anymore.
And in that moment
it didn't much matter
as long as it was   away.

It's not the time to stay in one place right now

The road's riddled
with storm after storm,
but I'll open my mind
and follow you everywhere.

You'll write your story
on clouds, lightning
as your pen.
I'll tapestry secrets
in the sad, silvery sky.

We'll murmur
into the collective wind
until it becomes a chorus

to change the view
speak up
alone... together
thundering a downpour of regret
in this human gridlock
of trembling hearts.

When this darkest night meets
the light of love,
we'll be the eye of the hurricane,
a garden of peace.

Star Sequence

"All I know is I saw stars." ~Maggie Martin

1. New York City
My childhood world –
always a wreath of fear
around my neck.
Adult anger a tightrope to tiptoe.

I dreamed of humming
electricity, streetlamps
as beacons. Emergency
vehicles racing on Broadway.

I grew up thinking
I could memorize the streets
of New York, make them my own.
If only I had followed
its lights earlier through the tunnel.

Now, in middle age, I still want
that city, how it never goes
completely dark.

2. Potter County
I found a piece of hope
when we stepped onto a deck
at the edge of a farmer's field
surrounded by a forest so deep it
held secrets that would
never see the light of day.

August's chill ran its fingers
down my spine. You held
my hand, said *look up*.

When I opened my eyes
I no longer knew
the hour or year or minute
or why we had driven
so far from the city.

All I knew was I saw stars.
And that was enough.

These Days

Fear is a heavy coat to wear
 day in, day out.

Let the fog hover.
Let the river flow.
Let the in-between of conversations
            be still.

Winter never got feet under it, never got full
sails up. Simply drifted away.

Now, a spring born of illness.

Welcome daffodils and dandelions.
            Anything willing to grow.

People will come together.
People will fall apart.

Like the hotel we lived in back in '82
until our new house was ready.
            Now empty. Broken windows. Tossed mattresses
            and dressers heaped in parking lot.

The rain spits as if it knows
its chance is only 50-50.

Stop spinning.

Let the wind chimes guide you.

Distance

1.
A rock mountain quietly sits
just out of reach of the shore.
Frothy foam hisses a goodbye.

2.
Climbing through cumulus,
again. The distance between
love & loss snatches a heartbeat.

3.
Cicada song, acoustic guitar
solo, frogs, cat shenanigans.
Clarity in midst of dense fog.

4.
August offers less light
waking up, more nights
of sweaters and wool socks.

5.
Fresh basil, pine, spearmint.
Reminders of a first whisper, his
hand on your back, that last kiss.

How long will it take you to learn that life doesn't wait?

for Marge

Sunflowers bow and you weep
at the beauty of nothingness. You run fast

and hard through the field. Kick off your
shoes and feel the love of summer dirt.

That's right – let it bathe your feet, find
its way under your toe nails. The angels

applaud. Wind pushes your hair
away from your eyes, trails it behind your body.

Feel the energy the closer you get to nowhere.
The moon's gone on vacation, you find your way

into and through tall, green stalks speaking what you
can not hear. Keep going. Straight to the center

of the Earth. Your broken heart is there.
It's patient, waiting for you to pick up the sea

glass buried where you never expected – cradled
in mountains kissing sky far inland from salt water.

The river turns its eyes on you. You stand at its edge
barefoot. You'll never forget the depths of its cold.

You always assumed everyone
would be there when you returned.

March 2020 – May 1994

The fever leads you in, away.
Days drench. Dry. Drench. Dry.
Sweat steals parts of your body.
Breasts deflate like balloons,
pancake against your ribs.

That last night you fed your last
child lying on the bedroom floor
your milk the color of coconut
trickling from corner of his
mouth. His brown eyes knowing.

X-Ray

1. Waiting
Postage-stamp waiting room
fringed with chairs
filled with people and pain.

Suspended TV
cornered
drones news
that raises blood pressure.

Fill-in new address.
Same insurance number, for now.
Check *separated*.

When I still lived at home
I wrenched my shoulder undressing
in our shared walk-in closet.

Months of aching I ignored
through the packing, the carrying
of boxes and clothes out through the garage,
up three flights of stairs.

The unpacking.

When I couldn't reach
into back seat
of my car for a backpack,
I finally surrendered to the pain.

2. Interior
The room is white.
I undress from waist up.
Paper gown scratches my skin.
Technician keeps eyes on her paperwork.
Asks my date of birth,
what hurts.

The tears are coming.

She retreats behind a radiation shield.
I stand directly in its path.

She is talking, but I only hear
the drone of the machine
that may shed light
on what's going on inside of me.
The tears are running.
She ignores them.
Tells me I can find my way out
after dressing.

I walk back through the crowded waiting room.
Eyes down.
Like there's something to be ashamed of.

3. Exterior
It's foggy and spitting rain.
The cold is descending.
I sit for a long stretch in my car
in the parking lot of a building
where I used to take our boys for well visits.
It's tucked away in the hills of the town
I so desperately wanted to call home.
The one I left when the weather was warm.

Rain-soaked windows.
The ache breaks open again.

Eve of an Ending

Winter held the morning air for an hour
before the sun turned it to spring.

I carried its scent with me as we flew
through the next night touching down

before Paris was fully awake. Before
anyone knew ink dissolved my marriage.

Very few want to face a city known
for love. I went praying for a new thirst –

one my ancestors knew well –
save yourself as we couldn't.

Search that soil for secrets.
Sleep. Eat. Walk. Repeat.

Your heart will heal. It's not too early
on the eve of an ending. A longing to be free.

Love is not born of sharp lines

Inspired by Dream Landscape #1 by Nancy Wells

Fall on fire.
Lightning flirting with night sky,
end of days bowing to twilight.

The sign language of a dancer –
            ebbing, flowing.

Greenland?

Glacial quiet of an apology, an inch of summer.

Snout of a dog.
Mother's arms,
child taken away – a cobalt pool of tears –

inlet of goodbye.

A stitch or two of a lie woven into the fabric of truth.

Corn ripe for picking.
                    Dandelion filaments flying.

The edge of thunder,
mountains prep for deluge.
A harvest moon telling us

            love is not born of sharp lines,
but infinite curves.

            There you are about to get lost at sea.
Here I am lost in a wheat field.

            This is how we rewrite history.

13 Ways

after Wallace Stevens

1.
Smooth Terrazzo. Grey
or brown, doesn't matter now.
Just your voice small
in cell pressed to my ear drowning
out flight-delay announcements.

2.
It took over a year
for you to speak your mind.
It took me 26.

3.
Silence lands
loudly on kitchen tile,
rough pattern
that always looked dirty
even when it wasn't.

4.
I know hard things.

5.
Throat a series of knots
words couldn't climb.
Just a sob. A few gasps.
Younger son's voice –
just breathe.

6.
With a knowing nod,
the bank employee
creates a new account
as I study the objects
on her desk, asks
if I want a lunch bag
or Tupperware.

7.
Wife and husband
for entire adult life.

8.
Never having lived
alone, I'm learning what
I want.

9.
Amazon suggests a family
plan to access books
on my Paper White.

10.
Beginnings of pulling
apart our life. Pieces
pliable as wet dough
while others brittle
like bleached hair.
Or cliché as a visit
to a mall Verizon store
in the middle of an afternoon.
One uncomfortable question
after another
but finally walking away
with a communication device
no longer a weapon.

11.
After eight years,
our conversations wobble
like a baby
giraffe learning to stand.

12.
I know sad things.

13.
Verb as in:
Leaving, left, separated, parting ways, uncoupling,
no longer united, unmarried, dissolved, breaking a family.

Opposite of:
Falling in, joining together, tethered,
coupled, paired off, given away, saving, trying, saved.

Had I known? Yes. Of course. Always yes.

Notes

"Love is not born of sharp lines" is an ekphrastic poem written about *Dream Landscape #1* by Nancy Wells.

"Ditto" is a found poem using words & phrases collected from AWP 2015 Book Fair marketing materials.

"I am not Dawn Colangelo anymore": "Patty's Charcoal Drive-In" is a poem by Barbara Crooker.

"It's not the time to stay in one place right now" is a found poem inspired by song titles and lyrics of Carole King's *Tapestry* and the NYC Women's March 2017.

"Timed Door" started as a found poem using words and phrases collected on the Minneapolis Skyway during AWP 2015, but then took a turn and became a completely different poem with few, if any, of the original words and phrases.

Acknowledgements

The author wishes to acknowledge the editors of the following magazines, anthologies, and journals where these poems originally appeared, sometimes in different versions and with different titles:

"After I Leave My Husband" – *New York Quarterly*

"Almost Spring" – *What Lies Behind the Frame, Bridgewater International Poetry Festival 2017 Anthology* (Unbound Content)

"Birthday Eve" – *Corvallis Advocate*

"Construction/Deconstruction" – *American Writers Review*

"Delta" – *Word Fountain*

"Ditto" – *SCOP*

"Elsewhere is where I want to be" – *Poets and Artists*

"Fusion" – *The Pine Cone Review*

"Good Girls" – *What Lies Behind the Frame, Bridgewater International Poetry Festival 2017 Anthology* (Unbound Content)

"Gone" – *Pennsylvania Bards Eastern PA Poetry Review 2021*

"Groceries for One" – *Verse-Virtual*

"Half Truths" – *San Pedro River Review*

"Heartbreak" – *Nobody Thoughts*

"Hiking" – *The Pine Cone Review*

"How long will it take you to learn life doesn't wait?" – *Anti-Heroin Chic*

"How to survive as a houseplant if you live with a beginner" – *Wild Roof Journal*

"I'm not Dawn Colangelo anymore" – *Paterson Literary Review*

"I woke up at 3 a.m. thinking I was somewhere else" – *Redheaded Stepchild Magazine*

"Independence" – *Keystone: Contemporary Poets on Pennsylvania* (The Pennsylvania University Press)

"Intersection" – *Corvallis Advocate*

"Let" – *Nobody Thoughts*

"Love is not born of sharp lines" – *SCOP*

"May Day" – *Corvallis Advocate*

"Meteor Shower" – *SWIMM*

"Monopoly" – *Bards Against Hunger Pennsylvania: An Anthology of Pennsylvania Poets*

"Ode to the First Place I Live Alone" – *New Square*

"Naming the Hurricane" – *I AM STRENGTH: True Stories of Everyday Superwomen* (Blind Faith Books)

"Naming Nail Polish" – *Nobody Thoughts*

"Shopping at Giant" – *Novus Literary and Arts Journal*

"Sin of Being Okay" – *Women Speak, Vol. 9* (Sheila-Na-Gig Editions)

"The House on Frink Street" – *Currents in the Electric City: A Scranton Anthology* (edited by Brian Fanelli and Joe Kraus, Belt City)

"we begin with pepper" – *Verse-Virtual*

"X-Ray" – *Pennsylvania Bards Southeast Poetry Review*

While the act of writing is a solitary pursuit that can often feel intimidating and isolating, the process of pruning and polishing a manuscript can be magical when writers ask for help. I am lucky and honored to have writer/editor friends and family who are generous with their time, talent, guidance, and patience.

Without them, this manuscript might still be swimming in a sea of doubt with drafts never able to catch a wave to shore.

A million thank yous, armfuls of love, and fierce respect for the following:

Monique Franz for believing in my words enough to publicly post that I would always have a publishing home at Kinsman Avenue Publishing.

Mischelle Anthony and Jennifer Judge Yonkoski, my sister poets and partners in all things poetic. Your careful reading and brilliant insights helped me shape these poems from rough drafts to finished poems. And your friendship helps me be a better person.

Cynthia Kolanowski for your spot-on suggestions, attention to detail, quiet encouragement as we walked circles around a conference table to order the collection, and your beautiful thoughts about my words.

Cynthia Atkins and Melissa Studdard for your generosity of spirit, time, and stunning words.

David Hicks, my friend and colleague, for inviting this poet to prose workshops and for your encouragement, suggestions, and brainstorming titles while walking back to campus from Abide Coffeehouse. And for consistently reminding me that I am a writer.

Barb Taylor, one of the most poetic prose writers I know, for feedback often shared by walking across the hall (long live Chapin memories), in late-night texts, and/or while on road trips as well as your laser-sharp editing and proofreading eye.

My twin, Donna Novicki, for taking that ever-important final proofreading lap.

Vicki Mayk for our conversations about writing over lunches, dinners, while planning Words in the Sand, and driving to and from the Jersey shore.

Craig Czury and the Monday Night Zoom group – David J. Bauman, Susan Bloch, Diane Funston, Angie Knott, Jennifer Maloney, Maggie Martin, Marge Merrill, Jane Sadowsky, Ruth Tonachel, and Scott W. Williams – for offering encouragement and holding space in which some of these poems first came to life.

Jenny Hill – creative force, poet, and arts educator – for offering workshops that sparked unexpected drafts.

Liz Faist and Gina Rice for the gift of co-teaching with you and how your art has impacted my writing.

Joe Carolan, Scott Carolan, Megan Carolan, Ann Marie Davis, Cecilia Delaney, and Abby Sheppard – who held me accountable during our Carolan Family Creatives virtual meetups and reminded me that in the midst of everyday life, I am a writer.

My family, immediate and extended, for a continuous stream of cheerleading, celebrating, and inspiration.

My sons, Ryan and Evan, for their unconditional love and putting up with a mom who writes about them.

And Nathan – for seeing what I could not, leading me to rethink some of these poems, which of course, made them better. But more than that, for loving and accepting all of me, all of the time.

About the Author

Dawn Leas (She/Her) is the assistant director of the Maslow Family Graduate Program in Creative Writing at Wilkes University. Her poetry has appeared in *New York Quarterly*, *The Paterson Literary Review*, *Literary Mama*, *The Pedestal Magazine*, *SWWIM*, and other journals. She is the author of *A Person Worth Knowing* (Foothills Publishing), *Take Something When You Go* (Winter Goose Publishing), and *I Know When to Keep Quiet* (Finishing Line Press).

In addition to her administrative and creative work, Leas is a writing coach, teaching artist, and editorial advisor for *River & South Review*. Outside of writing, she is a proud back-of-the-pack runner, hiker, salt-water lover, and mom of two grown sons.

Visit www.thehammockwriter.com.

.

www.ingramcontent.com/pod-product-compliance
Lightning Source LLC
Chambersburg PA
CBHW061709120626
46550CB00003B/1160